MW00389643

This book belongs to:

____

Made in the USA
Coppell, TX
10 May 2020

24745843R00066